Spitting Ink

James Finlay
Spitting Ink

Spitting Ink
ISBN 978 1 76041 740 6
Copyright © text James Finlay 2019
Cover image: Lisa Photios via Stocksnap

First published 2019 by
Ginninderra Press
PO Box 3461 Port Adelaide 5015 Australia
www.ginninderrapress.com.au

Contents

Not Yet a Poet	7
The Hue of Darkness	9
Autumn Army	10
West Terrace Parklands Forever	11
Every One of Them Wants My Money	13
The Tailored Jacket	15
The Colour of Death	18
It's Only Cannibalism If You Consider Them Human	19
Irreconcilable	20
The Crowd	22
You Will Know Me	23
5 List Poems	24
The House Is a Mess	26
Is it a Leaf or a Rat? (or Ode to Our Neighbour's Pool)	28
My Kind of Suicide	31
Crystallised	32
My Woman is Dead (and We Have Killed Her)	33
Wren	36
For the Days When My Flat Becomes a Monastery	37
The Morning After (A View From Pine Point)	38
The Incident With the Freight Train Near Port Pirie	40
Heaven is a Foyer in a Movie Theatre	41
Enraptured	42
The Utopian	44
Embers (In Memory of…)	46
Return To	49

Not Yet a Poet

I open my mouth
not to speak
but to listen.
Words will come when I have something to say.

But I do have something to say!
I can feel it there within me,
yet no words will come.

I am no poet –
a writer, I am,
a singer, I am,
a painter, I am,
a philosopher, I am,
but poet, no.

I am not among those so clearly ordained;
they who threw visions in ink and in voice,
they who poured out new ideas so fast they nearly drowned me,
whose combined effect was a cacophonous roar –
the wondrous swell of a tuning orchestra

and here I sit
able to speak of nothing
except the fact that I am unable to speak.

I open my mouth,
not to speak,
but to listen.
Words will come when there is something to say.

But there is too much to say!
I have so much anger and youth!

I have so many words
but I cannot tame them.
They say nothing except
'I have nothing to say,' and
'I am not yet a poet.'

It's funny.
Life is funny.
Life is so funny it makes me want to laugh,
laugh until I cry,
cry until I puke,
puke until I regurgitate my soul.

And perhaps my soul will land on the page,
there in a vomitous wreck of black ink;
there in words,
in verse,
in clarity.

Perhaps.

Perhaps then may I say,
'I am a poet
and I speak for I have something to say.'

The Hue of Darkness

In the secret hour I meet with myself,
Myself are you and I,
in the strange blue-green hue of darkness
where we meet.
You do not trust me any more
I understand
I have been unkind.

In the strange blue-green hue of darkness
blue spark.
I strike again.
Orange flame
eternalised briefly by a candle in a jar;
a haven.
Here the smallest flame is blinding.
Here where there is nothing but what the light touches.

Here where we meet.
Here where I meet.
Here in the secret hour.
Here in the strange glow of candle.
Puff.
Smoke.
Here in the strange blue-green hue of darkness.

Autumn Army

The ground is beautifully blanketed
in yellows, burgundies, and oranges
like littered phoenix feathers
still smouldering away
in spent brown embers.
The gutters run gold as if
some passing philanthropist
has been giving away
more coins than commoners can carry
or as if the sunshine has taken a holiday
in the stone gutters of North Adelaide
just to look up from the ground to the sky
for a change of scenery.

Then the hi-vis army rolls by
with the roar of mechanical wind
from three leaf blowers
and the beeping of a sweeper truck
screaming 'GET BACK! GET BACK!
LEST YOU BE SWEPT UP
IN THIS HURRICANE!
FOR THERE WILL BE
NO GUTTERSNIPES SPARED!'
as it sends feathers and coins
flying from whatever resting place
they had somehow found
amongst all the clamour and din
of this bizarre act of messy tidying,
this idiotic war of entropic displacement.

And now
there's just fucking leaves everywhere.

West Terrace Parklands Forever

Come one! Come all!
Come see the fantastic machines!
Now more expensive than ever!
The vehicular wonders of the modern age!
Updated! Upgraded!
As shiny as the glass buildings that
proudly line the city's edge
along the bustling terrace.

Yes, those glass buildings like
a great wall reflecting the image of
your own sorry vehicle as
you find yourself trapped
in a second-hand Toyota in
one of the four northbound lanes
going to work in a job that will
never earn the kind of
money you might need
to buy one of those marvellous machines.

They are the pinnacle of civilisation itself!
And surely it's better to be over
on the city side of West Terrace
than there on the parkland side
where the riff-raff remnants
of the old culture sleep in cheap tents
and cling to almost nothing at all;
where you can still touch the dirt;
where white people only go when they die.

And as the sun sets over the cemetery
the glass walls reflect the fate
of all who marvel at the machines.

But there is a moment,
one brief place, where the glass walls stop;
a little cottage
in the forest of beautiful roaring beasts
and they've painted another decade on their sign.

You see, selling cars to traffic
is not as sound a business move as
selling gravestones to a cemetery; and
a decade or two of prestige
can't stand up to
S.D. Tillett Memorials' 130 years of family tradition.

And no one will remember what car you drove
when you sleep
in the West Terrace parklands forever.

Every One of Them Wants My Money

He's oncoming foot traffic.
Our eyes lock.
He's all Velcro beard and a hand-me-down shirt.
I'm all tight-jeaned with a Doc Marten strut.

'Got any change?' he asks.
I don't.
It's a cashless society now.
We gave up a little security for a little convenience
and now these street-folk must suffer;
suffer for our convenience
bought with security.

And indeed we are insecure.
Black-hooded crims melting from the shadows
reaching out with needle fingers for our hard-earned taxpayer dollars,
dole-bludgers sponging,
immigrants stealing more than their fair share,
– these are the ones we watch for in a tireless vigil…

all the while white-collar punks
beat up economic runts
down at the stock exchange
and the rest of us hoard what we can of
empty promises and deferred payments.
'It's that or nothing, I'm afraid,' they say…

and now I and some guy
have our eyes locked like a loan contract.
This guy wants my money.
He's not the only one who does.
But he at least needs it.
He at least has the decency to ask.

No lies.
No deceit.

Just:
'Hey, can you spare some change?'
and I tell him,
'No, I'm sorry.'
And I am.
I am so deeply sorry.

The Tailored Jacket

Behind the glass
in the arsenal in Vienna
there's a jacket that's tailored for me.
The sleeves are long and narrow,
the waist comes in tight,
it looked like it would fit me just right

That was clear to see.

But what I couldn't see
was the thing I had come for;
that was being kept behind locked doors
as the museum was getting itself into gear
to mark the anniversary of a hundred years
since when in june of 1914
an archduke was shot by a guy like me
sparking two brutal wars
fought by guys like me.
Bullets shot
bombs dropped
hearts stopped
by guys like me –
young, idealistic, maybe twenty-three.

Some of the first blood shed
stained the archduke's uniform
still there and dry around the bullet holes, I'd heard
But that garment was somewhere I couldn't get at
so I was left to stare and react
to a somewhat different historical jacket
one, I admit, seemed tailored for me
with its sleeves long and narrow
and a waist brought in tight
and a swastika on the breast, all shiny and bright

And as the reflection of my face
floated above its neckline
like the ghost of someone killed by a guy like me
it was clear to see
that in another life, I could have been a Nazi
because, in truth, they were guys like me
young, idealistic, maybe twenty-three

There may not be enough Nazionalismus to my Sozialismus
but they are still my kind
and I must carry the weight of their guilt

For as long as whites are guilty
And I am white, then so am I guilty
For as long as men are guilty
And I am a man, then so am I guilty
For as long as the young are guilty
And I am young, then so am I guilty
For as long as the faithful are guilty
And I have faith, then so am I guilty
For as long as all are guilty
And I am one, then so am I guilty

After all
If the jacket fits
You might as well wear it.

The Colour of Death

If you drag a dagger down your brother's forearm
and let him bleed until his blood runs black with oil
do not be surprised when
he uses the black to paint himself a new flag to fly;
and do not be surprised when
he seeks to replace his lost red blood with yours
as he places his own dagger to your throat.

Does he look like a demon to you; as black as death?
Well, black does not mean death to him any longer, brother.
Not since you watched him explode with
your eyes hidden in the clear skies over his home.
Not since those eyes let it rain in the desert with
exploding hail, strobing red and white.

No, since that day death has not been coloured black,
nor has it been coloured khaki like your uniform.
For him, death is a pure sky blue
with a single white dove flying silently
waiting to drop a deadly message of peace and freedom.

Does it surprise you that your brother living under such skies
should become the demon in your bedtime stories?
And are you surprised to see your brother dressed
in the colour you call death?

It's Only Cannibalism If You Consider Them Human

When the government says,
>'We will eat all immigrants who reach our shore
>Do you still want them to come here?
>Or shall we turn them away?'

Do you let them die at home?
>– Or–

Do you let them be eaten?

Perhaps it is best to capitalise on the situation yourself
After all, immigrants are lean meat
Why not eat them?

Friends! There is another way!

When you're told your borders are being flooded
And your leaders give you a sound choice

The answer is clear:
>Eat the government.

Irreconcilable

must our first meeting
have been so violent?
must this rift between us
be so
                wide
and leave us so
irreconcilable?

it is too late for me to leave
      – to let your wounds heal
            themselves (in time)

the nation
who first sent me here
vowed to never let the sun
            set upon herself
and so it was
that she never saw the stars
amongst which you found such
            vivid dreams
     as you lay
     awake
     at night
     in wonder…

now it is too late
and I have no home
to which I may return
if you do not permit me
            to remain

for this land has claimed me too
the red
        of my blood
is coloured by the dust of
                this earth

the stars at which you have wondered
now, for me, point
                south and
                homeward

the stories
and songs
of this land
are the dust
in my veins

and though I am
in your scars
and though I have
stolen your children

I hope
through impossibility
that you can forgive me,
that we can both
be children of this land,

that we are not
indeed
irreconcilable.

The Crowd

In the crowd, I saw a face
In the face, I saw a crowd

You Will Know Me

you will know me
by the etching of
symbols in my flesh
that tell a thousand
riddles with no
answers and nothing
to connect them except
that I am
contained not in them
but in the spaces
between them

5 List Poems

5 Anxieties About List Poetry

1. That it's not really poetry
2. That I will expose too much of myself
3. That I will not expose enough of myself
4. That I will only be able to think of four items for a list
5. That I will feel compelled to add a sixth item to a list

A List of 5 Physical Insecurities

1. Weirdly skinny wrists
2. Veiny arms like something out of a science textbook
3. An irregular assortment of off-white teeth
4. Arched feet that are too small for my height
5. The slouchy posture I'm constantly trying to fidget out of

A List of 5 Totally Irrational Fears

1. The sudden bark of a dog from behind a fence
2. Going mad for a moment and stabbing myself with a kitchen knife
3. The spontaneous and violent explosion of electrical appliances
4. Cockroaches
5. A guitar string snapping and gashing my wrist

A Collection of 5 Dates of Personal Significance

1. 25th of October, 1990
2. 10th of December, 2011
3. Easter Weekend, 2007
4. 14th of October, 2007
4. 23rd of March, 2013

A Collection of 5 Cherished Possessions

1. A second-hand acoustic guitar
2. A stuffed toy dog
3. A grey blazer
4. A gold ring
5. A pair of used black Doc Marten boots

The House Is a Mess

When I was a child
and I'd get undressed
I'd leave clothes on the floor
so my room was a mess
this was a problem
I had to address
but I wasn't forced
so my room stayed a mess
and my mother did try
when we'd expect guests
to get me to clean
but my room stayed a mess
I'd never help clean
'less under duress
and the kitchen was filthy
and my mother would stress
and the toilet and bathroom
would never impress
so as you might guess
the whole house was a mess
and my mother would stress
until she would cry
and she'd get depressed
for the house was a mess
and the house was a mess
and my mother, depressed
she'd say 'I'm a mess!'

and she'd cry and she'd rest
and she'd rest and she'd rest
and she'd cry and obsess
that she'd be no good wife,
no good mother unless
she could finally address
the state of the mess
but she was depressed
too depressed and too stressed
and I would get stressed
because she was depressed
and both overwhelmed
the house stayed a mess
and on we'd obsess
staying stressed and depressed
and we'd never address
that the house is a mess
the house is a mess
the house is a mess
the house is a mess
the house is a mess
the house is a mess
the house is a mess
the house is a mess
the house is a mess
the house is a mess
the house is a mess
the house is a mess
the house is a mess

Is it a Leaf or a Rat?
(or Ode to Our Neighbour's Pool)

Tell me your secrets, LeafRat!
Rachel peers out from on high,
>> her heart palpitates
>> from new
>> anti-
>> depressants.

The cover came off our neighbour's pool
>> in the first week of August:
>> *There is nowhere in the world where August is*
>> *an appropriate time*
>>> *for the start of pool season.*

Our neighbour is like Gatsby.
> except,
> her parties only host tradie-
>> gardeners.
They haven't been since the LeafRat appeared.
It floated once,
> now it's sunk to the bottom
> (whatever it is)

> *Is that a tail? or a stem?*
It's too big and brown for the leaves of plants around.
But I don't see any rodent features.
> *It's sort of*
>> *just*
>>> *a*
>>>> *blob.*

It's been there for a couple of weeks now

              I think.

Why haven't they fished it out?
The gardeners are there all the time.

   Rachel is nervousenergetic from the meds.
So we walk
   and when she gets tired
we stop a moment
   and then, again
we stop again
   and when she gets dizzy
we sit
   and when she can't breathe
she passes out on the couch
   and when she passes out again
I call triple O:

Ambulance. South Australia. Adelaide.
She's gasping. Losing consciousness.
Sit her up.
Is she clammy? (check) *Yes.*
   (afterthought: *fit or tremors?*)
Distant sirens out the window.
Stay with her.
     Stay with me, Rach.
     Shake her shoulder.

She comes back:
>	Trouble speaking
>
>			at
>
>				all.

The ambos are chatty
>	and I don't panic.

Is that your pool?
>	*No*
>	*it might be our Leaf though*
>	*or certainly-not-our Rat.*

Later
>	she is ready to come home.

We drive in circles through the car park
>			via
>	cancelled dinner
>	and
>	a disabled elderly drunken walking frame
>		falling across the road with Amy's help.

So
Rachel comes home to *Holy Adam West, Batman!*
>	and she can talk again

>	and she is sad
because the pool is spotless.
>	and she knows they would not have fished it out
>			if it were a leaf.

My Kind of Suicide

My kind of suicide
ties no nooses,
slits no wrists,
consumes no poisons,
leaps from no great heights.

My kind of suicide
puts those scrawled notes
in a box under the bed.
It leaves the rest of the notebook blank.
It watches Netflix
and gets into all those shows I've been missing.
It focuses on my career
and works to earn
above all else.

My kind of suicide
remembers that phase I went through –
remembers it fondly –
as the folly it always was.

My kind of suicide
leaves no note,
has no witnesses.
It just slips away quietly
into a sensible oblivion
so no one knows I've even died.

My kind of suicide
leaves a breathing corpse
that never did finish writing that novel.

Crystallised

Like all men
        I am holding back
        my own body weight in tears
and I worry
        – if I let them go –
                that there will be nothing left
        of me
      except a puddle that
           turns into the crystallised
outline of
        a man
                  who once was.

My Woman is Dead (and We Have Killed Her)

I shovel soil.
>Flecks get caught in her lipstick.

I swear I didn't kill her.

They did!
>those ruthless, terrified boys!

Her favourite colour was pink
>(or was it mine?)
>but I persuaded it to green.

She has such a beautiful face
>– though no woman's face –
>>and I cover it with soil,

my shovel plunging into soft earth
as if into my own self,
and I bury her again.

I love her,
>but she must be buried;

buried along with all weeping –
buried along with all tenderness –
buried along with all vulnerability –
buried along with all joy.

So I shovel.
Her face disappears into the ground.

And the dam breaks
>into an endless torrent of abusive rage

because that's all those fuckers left me with.

No mourning this beauty with tears
        even though I love her so –
        even though she has my features –
        even though she is a part of me.

I pat the last of the soil into a small,
                neatly masculine,
                            mound.

I know they'd have killed us both
        if I hadn't let them kill her.
So I betrayed her –
                her blood on my hands
                and I cannot forgive myself.

I want to kill those who killed her;
        those who fear women so much that
            they would not
                even
                      allow me
                            to befriend one.

But I know to remain stoic.
But I cannot stay stoic any longer.

I cast the shovel down
        and it wounds the earth,

and then, finally, comes the flood.
    I weep.
And she is there, in the flood.

And now, with her white dress soiled,

    she rises
                despite everything

        to comfort and embrace me.

Wren

I died and I was weary
so I came back as a wren
and that life was brief
but I sang and I was beautiful

and life was fragile
so I came back as a carpenter
and life was crude
so I came back as a potter

and life was sparse
so I lived a thousand lives
and loved a thousand people
but half of them were you

and life became complicated
and I became weary
so I came back as a wren
and I sang and I was beautiful

For the Days When My Flat Becomes a Monastery

Today, a day of healing
A day of wearing black
The wind speaks through the treetops
The clouds will guard my back
I'll make a pot of coffee
I'll take off both my shoes
And dedicate this off'ring
This poem, to my Muse

The Morning After (A View From Pine Point)

I am the first to wake and my wife is snoring
Is this more tiredness, or
all headache and
the remainder of the night before not thrown purple into the toilet?

The lounge room is strewn with a thousand sleeping guitars
A hundred of which are a mistaken guitarist
(But how does he sleep in the full morning sun?)

The hem of my pyjama leg falls in love
with the dew of the grass outside
Which is a battlefield of
Wooden soldiers
A beer bottle
Someone's car keys
Plastic thrones
That fucking deflated volleyball
Now me too

A New Zealand poet at my fingertips
Weeds at my toes
Ocean at arm's length
       a swathe and vista
Warm sky too late for a sunrise

Some young fungi mourn and commiserate
                             heads bowed
Perhaps someone went over the edge
There is no guard rail and
the lawn slopes towards the drop

Perhaps I sang too loud
Perhaps my chords were wrong
Perhaps I didn't listen
Perhaps I offended

But they were all drunk too
The beautiful people
The games
The guitars
        now hungover from my discordant E major

And now
there is only the broken promises
of still-full wine glasses

The sober seagulls
        off to work
        gossiping
The sky
The sea
Me
Black Point reaching its arm around
        to embrace its old friends
The sky
The sea
Me

The Incident With the Freight Train Near Port Pirie

In another universe, we leave the beach a moment later.
In another universe, Nyasha panics.
In another universe, the car stalls in second gear.
In another universe, the car gets hit.
In another universe, I die with my next of kin.
In another universe, Angus receives the worst news.
In another universe, my last thought is of regret.
In another universe, the freight train horn still tolls as we cross the tracks
        just as it does in this universe
        where there are no bells to alert us
        where Nyasha calmly balances the clutch
        where the car moves away just barely in time
        where we stop just out of the way
        where the train pulls to a stop a mile down the line
        where we live
        where we pray together
        and cry
because in yet another universe
                            one of us looked.

Heaven is a Foyer in a Movie Theatre

Life is a film
that we have forgotten we are watching.
In the end
we will rise from our seats
and return to reality
as it really is,
while those who cannot believe
sit in the theatre
believing that it all ended
with a

sudden cut to black
and the credits rolling in silence.

Enraptured

On the days when I believe in God
on the days when I am bold enough to proclaim
that Utopia will indeed, someday, come

On the nights when the stars in the sky
sing with the moonlit water
and the twinkling city lights
hum along in the audience

On the days when the urban sprawl
is no more than an ink stain on the map
engulfed by the empty space around it
and when that empty space feels
unowned by any mortal

When the bitter tastes sting
and throw their colours on the page
and add to the fullness of
this fleeting life

When the single match
cannot hold out the dark,
yet I cannot help but be transfixed
upon its dying ember

When the bats at night
suddenly turn into the birds
that they were all along

When the face of the beloved
becomes strange
and in that strangeness
becomes new and wonderful

When I find myself
Me of all people
Here of all places
Now of all times
knowing that anywhere else
or anywhen else
could have suited me just fine in some other imagined life

I cannot help but think,
'No,
Not just anything,
Not in this life;
in this life, this is all that will do.'

And so
here I lie,
enraptured in the dark

The Utopian

I proclaim, as you did
        when you were as young and naïve
                as I am now,
    that
    Utopia will come.

The old will not even have the privilege
of forming the new foundation;
its ashes will be swept away
   and recycled into tissues
        to comfort those weeping from
            old miseries
                soon
                        to be
                              forgot
                                    ten.

We will not speak of clumsy tyrants.
      They will run their course
           and too, in time
                      dis
                          app
                                ear.

And even as I stand on tiptoes
looking to the sky
as the melted ice caps
      rise to my jawline
even then I will proclaim,
      Utopia will come.

For even then I must hope,
for I would rather have joy in my final days.
For if I do not hope
        why have I lived at all?

Embers (In Memory of…)

Written for the SIDS & Kids Memorial Service, 2018

For us, the living,
life cannot rest.

Some are stalked by strange
dark beasts.
Some have jaws full of teeth already
wrapped around their ankles.
All claw and kick and
scream in the face of death.

But not all battles
are won,
and not all fires
catch.

Here, now,
all we are left with is
a pile of unburned kindling and
promises yet unmade.

We have lost a child.
parents have lost a son, a daughter,
grandparents have lost a grandchild,
sons and daughters have lost a sibling
brothers and sisters have lost a niece, a nephew,
friends have lost the same.

Together, all
have lost a child.

But there was a time,
briefly,
when we still had.

We are strangely
fortunate to have borne witness to
the stars coalescing in such
a way that was so magnificent
that we could not help but be changed by it;
even if it were only a day;
even if it were only a moment;
even if only a spark.

Not all fires catch
and some rise up as embers in the night
and cool to ash before our eyes,
our faces sinking as we watch them float to ground.

And there are days
when our shoulders become earthen and
the ground seeps up into us to
draw us nearer so that
we stoop and cannot bare to walk.

But we will lift our eyes again.
Some other day we will lift them again.
We must.
We must, knowing we were faithful protectors; that
all that could be done was done; that
every ounce of frail, human energy was spent and
not one drop of our love was spared,

because they were ours
and they are still ours;
because they were here
and they are still here.

We loved them,
and we still love them,
and we will go on loving them
even if the only way we have left is
to remember them.

Return To

In death
our bodies will return to the womb of the earth,
warm and safe;
forever nurtured in a haven of dreamless sleep.
Only then will we find rest so wholesome
that it is finally enough.
'It is done,' we will say.
'No more.'

www.ingramcontent.com/pod-product-compliance
Lightning Source LLC
Chambersburg PA
CBHW062206100526
44589CB00014B/1970